THE UNION-CASTLE I

A Celebration in Photographs and Company Postcards

ALAN S. MALLETT

SHIP PICTORIAL PUBLICATIONS
1990

Cover: LLANSTEPHAN CASTLE by Maurice Randall (UCPSC 04/87)

Also by Alan S. Mallett
IDYLL OF THE KINGS (1980, World Ship Society)

By Alan S. Mallett and Andrew M. B. Bell
THE PIRRIE-KYLSANT MOTORSHIPS 1915–1932 (1984, Mallett & Bell Publications)

First Published in 1990 by Ship Pictorial Publications
3 College Close, Coltishall, Norfolk NR12 7DT

© Copyright Ship Pictorial Publications 1990

British Library Cataloguing in Publication Data
Mallett, Alan S.
  The Union-Castle Line: a Celebration in Photographs and Company Postcards

  ISBN 0 9516038 1 7

Ship Pictorial Series

Printed by Page Bros (Norwich) Ltd

INTRODUCTION

This is neither a Company nor a Fleet History. It is inspired by postcards issued by The Union-Castle Mail Steamship Company Limited between 1903 and 1967 collected by the author since he travelled to South Africa aboard CARNARVON CASTLE shortly after the Second World War.

Postcards were used by shipping companies to publicize their routes and of course their ships. Union-Castle produced an extraordinary variety using colour, photogravure, and after 1930, the familiar sepia tone. Within the basic design were minor differences in typeset and changes dictated by tonnage variations during an individual ship's career, totalling something over 500 different cards. All mailships built since 1890 and all passenger vessels serving since 1907 are included. However, to widen the scope a few photographs have been included to portray selected earlier vessels as well as some interior views, launches, and more recent vessels for which postcards were not issued. Union-Castle effectively ceased trading in the early 1980's and of all their ships only four remain, the former DUNNOTTAR CASTLE, KENYA CASTLE, and TRANSVAAL CASTLE, now engaged in full time cruising, whilst WINDSOR CASTLE is a permanent hostel ship on the Arabian coast. But the memory of the lavender hulled red and black funnelled liners which sailed like clockwork between Britain and South Africa for over a century will long remain.

Alan S. Mallett
Coltishall, Norfolk
September 1990

H.M. Queen Salote of Tonga, flanked by Captain Mayhew and Sir George P. Christopher, Union-Castle Chairman, aboard PRETORIA CASTLE II at the Coronation Review, 1953.   (Union-Castle Line)

A SHORT HISTORY OF THE UNION-CASTLE LINE

The application of the steam engine to ocean transport created inter alia a demand for Welsh coal at various English ports. Consequently Arthur Anderson, of the Peninsular and Oriental Steam Navigation Company, took the initiative in forming a company specifically to transport coal from South Wales to Southampton for use by his own vessels and those of the Royal Mail Steam Packet Company. The proposed name was "The Southampton Steam Shipping Company Limited" but when registered on 7th October 1853, the Company was entitled "The Union Steam Collier Company Limited". The likeliest reason for the change is that the first ship was named UNION, with four further vessels named after the constituent races forming the English, namely SAXON, BRITON, DANE and NORMAN. UNION was completed in 1854 and actually made a voyage or two in her intended service before the needs of the Crimean War called upon every available ship, and the new Union steamers were employed on P and O routes, and subsequently on war service. When peace came in 1856 there was no need to return to their planned service as this was now catered for, so the fleet was put out to charter and the Company renamed "The Union Steam Ship Company Limited".

The first Royal Mail steamship service to South Africa predated the Union Line. In 1851 the General Screw Steam Shipping Company Limited inaugurated a monthly service. However, their interests were more directed towards India and Australia than in the relatively poor Cape Colony. Sadly, their ambitions exceeded their profitability, and the service ceased in 1856. A service provided by W. S. Lindsay followed. Mr Lindsay was to become author of a monumental history of shipping, which enjoyed far greater success than his ship-owning venture, which ceased within a year.

Meanwhile the Union Line experienced considerable difficulty in finding profitable employment for its fleet. In 1857 a saviour appeared in the form of the Admiralty, seeking tenders for the Mail Service to the Cape. The Union Line tendered, and on 4th September learnt that it had been successful. On Tuesday 15th September DANE departed from Southampton for the Cape.

For 15 years the Union Line enjoyed a monopoly, despite the intrusion of a few would be rivals. Possibly the Company grew complacent. In 1872 came more serious opposition. A year previously a Mr George Payne founded the Cape and Natal Line. It had not enjoyed the best of luck, and as a final resort Mr Payne chartered two ships owned by Mr Donald Currie. They sailed for the Cape in early 1872, and whilst on voyage, Mr Payne had perforce to advise Mr Currie that he could not meet the charter terms.

Donald Currie was born in Greenock and brought up in Belfast. On leaving school he joined the Cunard Line and served them for 20 years rising to a senior position. He resigned in 1862 to form his own line of sailing ships running to India. An exceptionally astute businessman, he recognized that competition in the Indian trade was considerable, but that there was opportunity for his qualities in the Cape trade. Ultimately he claimed to have foreseen an excellent future for South Africa before he entered the trade. Certainly he realized that in chartering his ships to George Payne there was an element of risk. Currie came, saw, and eventually conquered. Relying on the fast passages of his first steamers to build up confidence, his

Castle Mail Packets Company secured a half share in the Mail Contract in 1876, run on a weekly basis. For the following 24 years there was a steady improvement in size and speed of ships, and quality of service, marked by a rivalry that at times passed well beyond bitterness, and always stoked up by Currie, ever an effective and active publicist.

Towards the end of the 1890's Currie faced serious problems. The Union Line had built new ships which utterly outclassed Currie's. Worse still, Currie's Castle Line was heavily reliant upon bank financing for its new buildings, for Currie had no intention of putting his personal wealth into that pot. In 1899 the Cape Government announced that the new contract would not be divided but issued "as a whole". To what extent this was influenced by Currie, who had strong personal contacts with the Cape ministers, is unknown. In the event it enabled Currie to invite the Union Line to join forces on 13th February 1900, thereby creating "The Union-Castle Mail Steamship Company Limited".

Currie, knighted in 1881, and now Sir Donald Currie GCMG, died in 1909. His last years had been clouded by dispute with the Cape Government over Deferred Rebates granted by the South and East African Shipping Conference (of which Union-Castle was the prime mover). In 1911 the new South African Government passed the Post Office Act precluding any line operating deferred rebates from participating in the Mail Contract. At this point Union-Castle managers, principally Sir Donald's sons-in-law, unwisely stood on their dignity and declined to budge. The impasse was resolved in April 1912 when the entire share capital was acquired by the Royal Mail Steam Packet Company and Elder, Dempster & Company Limited, headed by Sir Owen Cosby Philipps. For the following 19 years Union-Castle was a member of the Royal Mail Group which at its zenith controlled one fifth of Great Britain's merchant fleet. A combination of depressed trading conditions, over-buildings in the immediate postwar years, and excessive borrowing led to the collapse of the Group in 1931 and the regaining of the Union-Castle Line's independence. When Union-Castle had paid off onerous debts the way was open for a complete modernisation of the fleet, supervised by Sir Francis Vernon Thomson KBE, involving the building of three mail motorships, four intermediate motorships, seven cargo motorships, and substantial modernisation of five mailships and three intermediates, at a cost of over £10 million, completed by the end of 1938 when a new 14 day Mail service schedule was introduced requiring 19 knots speed.

Sir Vernon Thomson died in 1953, a few months before the Company celebrated its centenary. In 1956 Union-Castle Line and The Clan Line Steamers Limited combined to form the British & Commonwealth Shipping Company Limited, then under the direction of the Cayzer family. Three large Mail passenger ships, and two Mail cargo ships were built over the next 10 years, and the mail voyage time cut to eleven and a half days (22 knots). In late 1965 the sale of two mail ships to The South African Marine Corporation was approved. Oil price rises of the early 1970's and the impact of wide bodied jets played their part in speeding the demise of the Mail service, completed by the introduction of the container ships in 1977. On 20th October, SOUTHAMPTON CASTLE arrived at Southampton at the end of the final Mail sailing after 120 years and 35 days. Union-Castle remained for a few more years operating through Universal Reefers, a consortium formed with Safmarine, but by 1986 even this last vestige had passed into history. In a final irony, Union-Castle, now dormant, was embroiled for the second time in the largest British corporate failure to date, when on 2nd June 1990, its parent, British & Commonwealth Holdings plc, was placed in the hands of administrators.

NOTES TO THE ILLUSTRATIONS

1. Brief statistical particulars of ships illustrated are incorporated in the Index on pages 131 to 136.

2. All illustrations are from the author's collection.

3. The author and publishers wish to thank the suppliers of photographs used for permission to reproduce. Credits are shown in situ. Other illustrations are from postcards produced by the Union-Castle Line, and the Union-Castle Postcard Study Circle catalogue number is stated. Information about the Study Circle may be obtained by sending a stamped addressed envelope to UCPSC, Hill House, Ramsey, Nr Harwich, Essex, CO12 5LN.

   The World Ship Photo Library is the collection of the World Ship Society. Information about the Society may be obtained by sending a Stamped addressed envelope to Dept. UC, 28 Natland Road, Kendal, Cumbria, LA9 7LT.

   Upper Clyde Shipbuilders records held by Strathclyde Regional Archives are reproduced by courtesy of the Principal Archivist and by permission of the Keeper of the Records of Scotland.

4. A Roman numeral following a ship's name indicates the first (second, etc) vessel of that name in the fleet.

5. Dates following the ship's name indicates the period during which the vessel concerned was owned or operated by the Union, Castle, or Union-Castle Lines. Unless specifically stated ships were completed in the opening year of service for the Union-Castle Line.

6. It should be noted that in certain cases tonnage shown on the postcards differs from those shown in the Index. This is caused by modifications to ships during the course of their careers.

7. The term "class" indicates that the ship in question is one of several ships of broadly similar design but subdivided into a number of smaller groups. The term "sister ship" indicates vessels built to the same dimensions, specifications and power which are generally similar but not necessarily identical in appearance and layout.

8. For convenience and brevity the following abbreviations are used:

   The Union-Castle Mail Steamship Company Ltd = Union-Castle Line.

   The Union Steam Ship Company Ltd = Union Line.

   The Castle Mail Packets Company (Ltd after 1881) = Castle Line.

   The South African Marine Corporation Ltd = Safmarine.

   The Clan Line Steamers Ltd = Clan Line.

   Harland & Wolff Ltd = Harland & Wolff.

   Barclay, Curle & Co Ltd = Barclay Curle.

   The Fairfield Shipping & Engineering Company Ltd = Fairfields.

SAXON II (1863–1876)

(The late P. A. Vicary)

Built by Day, Summers and Co. Southampton, for the Union Line. Set a new record of 31 days from Plymouth to the Cape on her maiden voyage, and achieved 28½ days in 1865. Sold in 1876, renamed BENGUELLA. 1890 Foundered 24th June, 250 miles off Lisbon.
Sister ship: ROMAN I

Roman

ROMAN I (1863–1889) (World Ship Photo Library)

Built by C Lungley, Deptford for the Union Line. 1872 lengthened, and engines compounded. Served as a mailship, extra ship, and on the Southampton - Hamburg feeder service until sale in 1889 to Turkish interests. Renamed ADANA, finally sunk at Izmir in 1912 as a blockship.
Sister ship: SAXON II

GOTHLAND (1872–1876)

(Nautical Photo Agency)

Built 1871 by J & G Thomson, Glasgow, for Leith, Hull & Hamburg Steam Packet Co Ltd, 1872, and chartered to George Payne & Co. 1876 Returned to the North Sea service. 1922 Sold and renamed **TRUDE BREMER**. 1924 Broken up in Germany.

EDINBURGH CASTLE I (1872–1880) (Nautical Photo Agency)

Built by Robert Napier & Co, for the Castle Line. 1880 Sold and renamed ESPANA. 1898 Broken up April at Marseilles.
Sister ship: WINDSOR CASTLE I

FLORENCE (1873–1889) (National Maritime Museum)

Built 1865 by Robert Napier & Co, for the Leith Hull & Hamburg Steam Packet Company. 1873 Acquired by Donald Currie, lengthened, and engines compounded. Served on S. African coast until sale in August 1889 to Turkish owners, renamed KRITI, later CRETE, and in 1912 GUIRRIT. 1919 Broken up. The only clipper stemmed steamer owned by Donald Currie.

ANGLIAN II (1873–1894)   (World Ship Photo Library)

Built by Aitken & Mansell, Glasgow, for the Union Line. 94 First, 50 Second and 100 Third class passengers. 1886 Engines tripled and transferred from Mail to coastal service. 1894 Sold to Huddart Parker Ltd, 1913 hulked at Adelaide, and 1933 scuttled off Sydney Heads on 2nd August.

DUNROBIN CASTLE (1876–1893)

(A. Duncan)

Built by R Napier & Sons, for the Castle Line, the first "Castle" specifically designed for the South African service. 100 First, 50 Second, 100 Third class passengers. 1893 Sold 25th October renamed NOTRE DAME DE SALUT. 1914 Broken up at Genoa in January.

GRANTULLY CASTLE I (1880–1896)   (Nautical Photo Agency)

Built by Barclay Curle, Glasgow, for the Castle Line. 120 First, 100 Second and 160 Third class passengers. 1887 Engines tripled. 1896 Sold to Booth Steamship Company Ltd, renamed AUGUSTINE. 1912 Broken up September at Falmouth. Sister ship: KINFAUNS CASTLE I

TROJAN (1880–1900) (Ship Society of S. Africa)

Built by J & G Thomson, Glasgow, for the Union Line. Reputedly the second ship afloat to be lit by electricity (one light bulb in the saloon). 116 First, 90 Second and 50 Third class passengers. Engines tripled in 1887. Served as hospital ship 1899–1900. 1901 sold to Elder, Dempster & Co. Ltd. Resold to French owners 1904 broken up at Marseilles.

ATHENIAN (1882–1897)

Built by Aitken & Mansell, Glasgow, for the Union Line 150 First, 50 Second and 130 Third class passengers. On 22nd October 1882 became first ship to enter Robinson Dry Dock at Cape Town. 1886 Engines tripled. 1897 Sold to Canadian Pacific Railway Co. Ltd. 1907 Sold 14th September and broken up in Japan.
Sister ship: MOOR

ROSLIN CASTLE II (1883–1905)   (A. Duncan)

Built by Barclay Curle, Glasgow, for the Castle Line. 158 First and 84 Second class passengers. 1888 Lengthened and engines tripled and reduced homeward record to 17 days. Sold January 1905 to German owners, renamed REGINA, and chartered as a storeship for the Imperial Russian Fleet on its voyage from the Baltic to the Far East. March 1905 ran aground off Mozambique, and eventually broken up at Genoa in May 1907.
Sister ships: NORHAM CASTLE & HAWARDEN CASTLE

UNION-CASTLE LINE ROYAL MAIL STEAMER "PEMBROKE CASTLE"

PEMBROKE CASTLE II (1883–1906)   (UCPSC 01/01)

Bought on the stocks by the Castle Line. Built by Barrow Shipbuilding Co. Ltd, the only pre 1900 "Castle" completed outside Scotland. Famed for her inaugural cruise to North Scotland and Copenhagen when 29 European royalties lunched aboard with WE Gladstone. Queen Victoria was not amused. Usually employed as an Extra service ship. 1906 Sold to Turkish Government, renamed TIRI-MUJGIAM and sunk near Samsoun in August 1915 by the Russian fleet.

DUNOTTAR CASTLE I (1890–1913)

(World Ship Photo Library)

Built by Fairfields for the Castle Line. The first twin funnelled "Castle". 168 First, 92 Second and 100 Third class passengers. Broke the Cape record on her maiden voyage and subsequently improved on her timings. 1913 Sold to the Royal Mail Steam Packet Co. to continue her cruising career as CARIBBEAN. 1915 Foundered 27th September off Cape Wrath in heavy weather whilst on naval service.

SCOT (1891–1905) (Union-Castle Line)

Built by W. Denny & Bros, Dumbarton for the Union Line. Shown in her original livery, changed after a few voyages to white hull. 212 First Class, 105 Second and 108 Third Class passengers. The first twin screw mailship. Set a record of under 14 days 19 hours in 1893 which stood for 43 years.

SCOT (1891–1905)   (J. G. Callis)

Shown after lengthening in 1896. 1905 Sold and renamed OCEANA. Resold in 1911 and 1914. 1916 Sold and renamed ALFONSO XIII. 1923 Renamed VASCO DA GAMA. 1927 March broken up in Italy.

UNION-CASTLE LINE INTERMEDIATE STEAMER "GOTH." 4,778 TONS.

GOTH (1893–1913)   (UCPSC 02/47)

Built by Harland & Wolff for the Union Line. 50 First, 60 Second and up to 500 Third class passengers. Sold 9 October 1913 to Royal Mail Steam Packet Co, renamed COBEQUID. 1914 Ran ashore 13 January on Trinity Ledge, Bay of Fundy, and became a total loss.
G Class First Group
Sister ships: GAUL & GREEK

TANTALLON CASTLE II (1894–1901)

(World Ship Photo Library)

Built by Fairfields for the Castle Line. 200 First,150 Second and 150 Third Class Passengers. She was the first mailship fitted with Quadruple Expansion engines. 1901 Ran ashore 7th May off Robben Island whilst entering Table Bay and despite strenuous efforts became a total loss.

UNION-CASTLE LINE ROYAL MAIL STEAMER "GUELPH."

GUELPH (1894–1913)
(UCPSC 03/33)

Built by Harland & Wolff for the Union Line. A slightly enlarged version of GOTH (qv) with like passenger accommodation and similar service. 1913 Sold to Royal Mail Steam Packet Co. and renamed CARAQUET. 1923 Ran ashore 25th June off Bermuda and became a total loss.
G Class Second Group

LAUNCH OF THE S.S. NORMAN AT HARLAND AND WOLFFS SHIPYARD, BELFAST, 19.7.91. R.WELCH.
LENGTH, 515. 7,600.I.H.P. WEIGHT WHEN LAUNCHED 4,883. TONS. FINISHED, 7000 TONS.

NORMAN II (1894–1926)   (Harland & Wolff)

Built by Harland & Wolff for the Union Line. NORMAN was regarded as a miniature version of the highly successful White Star Liners designed by Sir William Pirrie. Launched 19th July 1894, she made her maiden voyage 10th November.

UNION-CASTLE LINE ROYAL MAIL STEAMER "NORMAN." 7,537 TONS.

NORMAN II (1894–1926) (UCPSC 07/45)

150 First, 100 Second, 100 Third plus 300 Open Berth Passengers. Served as a mail ship until 1910 and again 1919–1921. In August 1914, she transported the first of the British Expeditionary Force to France. Her last years were on the Round Africa Service. The first ever cinema show at sea was given by Carl Hertz aboard NORMAN in March 1896. 1926 broken up at Morecambe.

INTERMEDIATE STEAMER "DUNVEGAN CASTLE."   6,124 TONS.

DUNVEGAN CASTLE I (1896–1923)   (UCPSC 11/96)

Built by Fairfields for the Castle Line. 287 First, 96 Second and 130 Third Class Passengers. 1902 7th October struck the Elbow berth, Victoria Dock Cape Town whilst entering harbour, causing considerable damage to the stonework but little to herself. Served as Mailship until 1910 and again during the war, also as a Hospital ship, and on the East African service 1912–1914 and postwar. 1923 Sold 12th December for breaking up in Germany.

UNION-CASTLE LINE ROYAL MAIL STEAMER "TINTAGEL CASTLE"

TINTAGEL CASTLE I (1896–1912) (UCPSC 01/31)

Built by Fairfields, Glasgow for the Castle Line. 71 First 98 Second and 150 Third Class passengers. Intermediate service.
1912 sold and renamed LIGER. 1923 broken up.
Sister ship: AVONDALE CASTLE

UNION-CASTLE LINE TO SOUTH AND EAST AFRICA

INTERMEDIATE STEAMER "GASCON." 6,341 TONS.

GASCON (1897–1928) (UCPSC 09/96)

Built by Harland & Wolff for the Union Line. 78 First, 118 Second and 180 Third Class Passengers. Served mainly on the West coast Intermediate service, and from 1914–1918 as Hospital ship. 1928 Broken up at Inverkeithing.
G Class third group
Sister ships: GAIKA & GOORKHA

UNION-CASTLE LINE INTERMEDIATE STEAMER "GAIKA." 6,392 TONS.

GAIKA (1897–1929) (UCPSC 02/47)

Built by Harland & Wolff, Belfast for the Union Line. Passenger accommodation as GAIKA. Served as troopship 1916–1918. 1922 ran ashore 16th April in Three Anchor Bay, near Cape Town, but soon refloated. 1929 Broken up in Italy.
G Class Third Group
Sister ships: GASCON & GOORKHA

UNION-CASTLE LINE INTERMEDIATE STEAMER "GOORKHA." 6,300 TONS.

GOORKHA (1897–1926) (UCPSC 08/63)

Built by Harland & Wolff Ltd, Belfast. Passenger accommodation as GAIKA. The first Union Liner with stockless anchors (unlike her two sisters). Served mainly on the West coast Intermediate service with some round Africa voyages postwar. War service was as a Hospital ship. 1917 Mined 17th October on passage Salonika to Malta. 1926 broken up in Italy.
G Class Third Group
Sister ships: GASCON & GAIKA

BRITON III (1897–1926)   (Harland & Wolff)

Built by Harland & Wolff for the Union Line. 260 First 192 Second, 186 Third and 300 Steerage passengers. The view shows the First Class Drawing Room. 1926 broken up in Italy.

UNION-CASTLE LINE STEAMER "CARISBROOK CASTLE." 7,594 TONS.

CARISBROOKE CASTLE II (1898–1922)   (UCPSC 04/65)

Built by Fairfields Glasgow, for the Castle Line. The final single screw mailship. Faster than all the other mailships except SCOT. Served mainly on Royal Mail service until 1910, thereafter East African service. Wartime use was as a Hospital ship. 1922 broken up in Germany.

INTERMEDIATE STEAMER "BRAEMAR CASTLE." 6.318 TONS.

BRAEMAR CASTLE I (1898–1924)   (UCPSC 11/96)

The last and best of the Intermediates built for the Castle Line, by Barclay Curle, Glasgow. From 1909 almost exclusively used for trooping. 1916 23rd November damaged by mine in the Mykoni Channel, close to where BRITANNIC succumbed two days earlier. 1918 Served as Base Hospital at Murmansk during the Anglo-French intervention. 1924 broken up in Italy.

UNION-CASTLE LINE INTERMEDIATE STEAMER "GLENGORM CASTLE." 6,769 TONS.

Norman. D. Hollnosk.

GERMAN II / GLENGORM CASTLE (1898–1930)

(UCPSC 05/48)

Built by Harland & Wolff, Belfast for the Union Line. 90 First Class, 120 Second Class passengers. Intermediate service 1899–1914 and 1926–1930. Wartime Hospital ship (renamed GLENGORM CASTLE 14th September 1914). Postwar served as troopship until 1925, with one Mail sailing on 11th November 1921 intervening. This postcard dates from that period. 1930 broken up in the Netherlands.

G Class Fourth Group

Sister ships: GALICIAN/GLENART CASTLE & GALEKA

UNION·CASTLE LINE ROYAL MAIL STEAMER "KINFAUNS CASTLE." 9,656 TONS.

KINFAUNS CASTLE II (1899–1927)

(UCPSC 19/85)

Built by Fairfields, Glasgow, for the Castle Line. 266 First, 171 Second 148 Third Class Passengers. Served as Armed Merchant Cruiser and Troopship during the War. 1922 rescued passengers and crew of the German ss HAMMONIA when the vessel foundered in heavy weather in the Bay of Biscay. 1927 broken up in Holland.
Sister ship: KILDONAN CASTLE

UNION-CASTLE LINE ROYAL MAIL STEAMER "KILDONAN CASTLE." 9,692 TONS.

KILDONAN CASTLE (1899–1931)   (UCPSC 11/45)

Built by Fairfields Glasgow, for the Castle Line. Completed as a troopship. 266 First, 171 Second 198 Third Class Passengers. Mail Service from 1901. During the War she served as a Hospital ship and Armed Merchant Cruiser. 1917 January embarked the Allied Mission to Russia, returning to Scapa on March 2nd, shortly before the outbreak of the Russian Revolution. Her final 5 years were spent mainly in reserve. 1931 broken up at Stavanger.
Sister ship: KINFAUNS CASTLE II

GALEKA (1899–1916)   (Capt. J Wilford)

Built by Harland & Wolff, Belfast for the Union Line. Passenger accommodation as GERMAN II. Intermediate service until 1914, thereafter trooping 1914–1915 and from June 1915 Hospital ship. 1916 Mined 28th October, 5 miles NW Cape la Hogue, drifted ashore and became a total loss, as shown.
G Class Fourth Group
Sister ships: GERMAN II/GLENGORM CASTLE & GALICIAN/GLENART CASTLE

UNION-CASTLE LINE ROYAL MAIL STEAMER "SAXON"

SAXON IV (1900–1935)   (UCPSC 23/31)

Built by Harland & Wolff, Belfast, the first mailship completed for the Union-Castle Line. 310 First, 203 Second and 286 Third Class Passengers. Served as a Mailship until 1931, and after one Intermediate sailing, laid up. 1935 Sold 9th April for breaking up at Blyth. A highly successful career marred only by a bunker fire on 14th August 1921 on voyage to Cape Town which delayed her, and passengers including General Smuts a week.
Saxon Class First Group
Sister ship: WALMER CASTLE II

SAXON IV (1900–1935)   (Harland & Wolff)

The opulence of the First Class Drawing Room aboard BRITON (qv) contrasts with the stark comforts of a Third Class cabin aboard SAXON. However, be it noted that the owners did provide the bedding for passengers!

UNION-CASTLE LINE ROYAL MAIL STEAMER "GALICIAN."

GALICIAN/GLENART CASTLE (1900–1918)   (UCPSC 01/25)

Built by Harland & Wolff, Belfast. Passenger accommodation as GERMAN II. Intermediate service. 1914 Intercepted 15th August by SMS KAISER WILHELM DER GROSSE near Teneriffe but released the next day on account of the women and children on board. Renamed GLENART CASTLE. 1916 rescued 476 survivors from ss WELSH PRINCE and ss ARABIA after they had been torpedoed off Cape Matapan. 1918 torpedoed and sunk 26th February by UC56 off Lundy whilst fully illuminated as a Hospital ship, 162 lives lost.
G Class Fourth Group
Sister ship: GERMAN II/GLENGORM CASTLE

AROS CASTLE (1901–1917)   (Tom Rayner Collection)

Built by Barclay Curle, Glasgow. One of four cargo only vessels acquired in anticipation of a trading bonanza in the wake of the Boer War, which failed to materialize. Served mainly on the New York–South Africa service. Torpedoed 21st November 1917, 300 miles W by S from Bishop Rock, and sunk with loss of two lives.

CAWDOR CASTLE (1902–1926)   (National Maritime Museum)

Built by Barclay Curle, Glasgow, one of five vessels intended as predominantly cargo carriers with immigrant accommodation and 20 First and 20 Second Class passengers. All four vessels came to untimely ends, CAWDOR CASTLE, having escaped attack by a German submarine on 13th December 1915, running ashore in Conception Bay, S W Africa, on 30th July 1926. After the war her hull was painted black.
Sister ships: ALNWICK CASTLE, BERWICK CASTLE, NEWARK CASTLE

CLUNY CASTLE II (1903–1924)   (Ship Society of S Africa)

Built by Barclay Curle, Glasgow. Intended as an immigrant carrier. 8 First Class, 20 Second Class and 140 Third Class Passengers. 1924 Sold to Bullard King & Co Ltd on the 17th December, renamed UMKUZI. 1938 Sold for demolition in July.
Sister ship: COMRIE CASTLE

ROYAL MAIL STEAMER "WALMER CASTLE."   12,546 TONS

WALMER CASTLE II (1902–1932)   (UCPSC 21/91)

Built by Harland & Wolff, Belfast, originally to be named CELT. 336 First, 174 Second and 244 Third Class Passengers. Differed in detail from SAXON and succeeding mailships. Her voyage of 49 days from Tilbury to the Cape in January / February 1917 was the lengthiest mail sailing by Union-Castle albeit caused by wartime exigencies. 1930 Withdrawn, 1932 broken up at Blyth.
SAXON class First group
Sister ship: SAXON IV

ROYAL MAIL STEAMER "ARMADALE CASTLE." 12,973 TONS.

ARMADALE CASTLE (1903–1936)
(UCPSC 30/92)

Built by Fairfields, Glasgow. 350 First, 200 Second 270 Third Class Passengers. 1904 On 26th June became the first mailship to enter Durban Harbour. Wartime service was as an Armed Merchant Cruiser, notably in the S W Africa campaign in 1914.
SAXON Class Second group
Sister ship: KENILWORTH CASTLE II

UNION-CASTLE LINE TO SOUTH AND EAST AFRICA.

ROYAL MAIL STEAMER "ARMADALE CASTLE." 12,999 TONS.

ARMADALE CASTLE (1903–1936)   (UCPSC 02/138)

This 1933 postcard shows ARMADALE CASTLE with fully enclosed wheelhouse fitted after her 1919 refit. 1935 Withdrawn December. 1936 February hastily recommissioned to replace WINCHESTER CASTLE after that vessel ran ashore. August broken up at Blyth.

UNION-CASTLE LINE TO SOUTH AND EAST AFRICA.

INTERMEDIATE STEAMER "DURHAM CASTLE." 8,240 TONS.

DURHAM CASTLE (1904–1939)   (UCPSC 16/139)

Built by Fairfields, Glasgow. First of three distinctly superior intermediates. 230 First, 270 Third and 300 Steerage Class Passengers. West coast intermediate service until 1910, extended to Mombasa until 1914. Postwar service on the West Coast intermediate service to Beira until 1931, thereafter the Round Africa service. 1939 Sold June for demolition. Requisitioned for service as Depot ship, but mined and sunk 26th January 1940 off Cromarty whilst in tow for Scapa Flow. Sister ships: DOVER CASTLE II & DUNLUCE CASTLE

UNION-CASTLE LINE INTERMEDIATE STEAMER "DOVER CASTLE."

DOVER CASTLE II (1904–1917)   (UCPSC 14/20)

Built by Barclay Curle, Glasgow. West Coast Intermediate service. 230 First, 270 Third Class and 300 Steerage Passengers.
Served as Hospital ship from August 1915. October 1916 rescued 302 survivors from ss FRANCONIA torpedoed 195 miles
East of Malta, 1917 torpedoed 26th March by UC 67 north of Cap de Fer.
Sister ships: DURHAM CASTLE & DUNLUCE CASTLE

UNION-CASTLE ROYAL MAIL STEAMER "KENILWORTH CASTLE." 12,975 TONS.

KENILWORTH CASTLE II (1904–1936)   (UCPSC 22/143)

Built by Harland & Wolff, Belfast. Passenger accommodation as ARMADALE CASTLE. 1918 4th June, 35 miles out of Plymouth en route to the Cape collided with H M Destroyer RIVAL, severing that vessels stern and releasing primed depth charges which detonated with devastating effects. Fortunately it proved possible to beach her. 1936 Broken up from December at Blyth.
SAXON Class Second group
Sister ship: ARMADALE CASTLE

THE UNION-CASTLE LINE INTERMEDIATE STEAMER "DUNLUCE CASTLE." (8,130 TONS)

DUNLUCE CASTLE (1904–1939)   (UCPSC 06/110)

Built by Harland & Wolff Belfast, Intermediate service 1904–1914 and 1920–1931 thereafter Round Africa. Passengers as DOVER CASTLE II. Trooping and Hospital ship 1914–1919. 1910 inaugurated the extended Intermediate service to Mombasa. 1925 took a Mail sailing on 16th October during seamen's strike. 1939 sold June for demolition but requisitioned for service as Depot Ship mainly at Scapa. 1945 demolition commenced at Inverkeithing.

INTERMEDIATE STEAMER "GRANTULLY CASTLE." 7,612 TONS.

GRANTULLY CASTLE II (1910–1939)   (UCPSC 13/134)

Built by Barclay Curle, Glasgow. 75 First, 110 Second and 200 Third class passengers. Served as a Hospital ship in Dardanelles campaign, during which time the poet Rupert Brooke was a patient shortly before his death. 1939 sold for demolition at Bo'ness and arrived 20 August.
G CASTLE class First group
Sister ship: GARTH CASTLE II

BALMORAL CASTLE II (1910–1939)   (Strathclyde Regional Archives)

Built by Fairfields, Glasgow, and shown immediately prior to launching on 13th November 1909. 320 First, 220 Second and 250 Third Class passengers. In September 1910 served as a Royal Yacht to carry TRH The Duke and Duchess of Connaught to inaugurate the first Parliament of the Union of South Africa. BALMORAL CASTLE was the first Cape mailship to be fitted with radio.
SAXON Class Third Group

Sister ship: EDINBURGH CASTLE II

BALMORAL CASTLE II (1910–1939)

(Strathclyde Regional Archives)

BALMORAL CASTLE immediately following her launching. After trooping service in the First World War she was selected to carry members of the Houses of Parliament to the Royal Naval Review at Spithead on the 21st July 1919, thereafter returning to the mail service. Her sale, on 20th July 1939 to J Cashmore, Newport, for demolition was after a three month lay-up at Government behest.

UNION-CASTLE LINE TO SOUTH AND EAST AFRICA.

INTERMEDIATE STEAMER "GARTH CASTLE." 7,625 TONS.

GARTH CASTLE II (1910–1939)

(UCPSC 05/139)

Built by Barclay Curle, Glasgow. Passenger accommodation as GRANTULLY CASTLE. Served as Fleet Hospital at Scapa in the war. 1926 ran ashore 25th March in English Bay, Ascension, but refloated 8 feet down by the head. 1939 sold 20th June, for demolition at Blyth.
G CASTLE Class First Group
Sister ship: GRANTULLY CASTLE II

THE UNION-CASTLE ROYAL MAIL STEAMER "EDINBURGH CASTLE." 13,329 TONS.

EDINBURGH CASTLE II (1910–1941) (UCPSC 23/153)

Built by Harland & Wolff, Belfast. Served throughout the First World War as an Armed Merchant Cruiser. Passenger accommodation as BALMORAL CASTLE, but reduced in both ships after 1920. Designated in July 1938 for retention as reserve mailship. Laid up 1939 but requisitioned by the Admiralty. Sale finally agreed in June 1941. Paid off 15th May 1944 and rejected for use as troopship. 5th November 1945 towed out of Freetown and sunk by gunfire from HMS FAL and HMS PORTCHESTER CASTLE.

SAXON Class Third Group
Sister ship: BALMORAL CASTLE II

INTERMEDIATE STEAMER "GLOUCESTER CASTLE." 8,006 TONS.

GLOUCESTER CASTLE (1911–1942) (UCPSC 03/139)

Built by Fairfields, Glasgow. First of an ill fated trio. 87 First, 130 Second and 195 Third Class Passengers. 1917 torpedoed 31st March in the English Channel whilst serving as Hospital ship, but beached and repaired. Principally engaged on West coast intermediate service. 1939 Laid up, but recommissioned, despite her lack of speed. 1942 sunk on 15th July by the German surface raider MICHEL near the equator, with tragic loss of life, the survivors eventually being taken to Japan.
G CASTLE Class Second Group
Sister ships: GUILDFORD CASTLE & GALWAY CASTLE

UNION-CASTLE LINE INTERMEDIATE STEAMER "GUILDFORD CASTLE." 7,995 TONS.

GUILDFORD CASTLE (1911–1933) (UCPSC 15/63)

Built by Barclay Curle, Glasgow. Passenger accommodation as GLOUCESTER CASTLE. 1918 Attacked 10th March by submarine (believed U-110) whilst serving as Hospital ship, one torpedo missed and another failed to explode. 1933 sank in Elbe on 1 June after being rammed by ss STENTOR, both vessels being in charge of their German pilots.
G CASTLE Class Second Group
Sister ships: GLOUCESTER CASTLE & GALWAY CASTLE

UNION-CASTLE LINE INTERMEDIATE STEAMER "GALWAY CASTLE." 7,988 TONS.

GALWAY CASTLE (1911–1918)

(UCPSC 02/63)

Built by Harland & Wolff, Belfast. Passenger accommodation as GLOUCESTER CASTLE. Intermediate service until 1914, trooping 1914–1915 thereafter on wartime mail service. 1916 bombed by German aircraft 3rd August off Gull lightship but missed. 1917 12th October ran ashore off East London refloated some days later. 1918 12th September torpedoed by U 82 200 miles South of Lands End, sank 15th September. 150 lives lost out of 950.
G CASTLE Class Second Group
Sister ships: GLOUCESTER CASTLE & GUILDFORD CASTLE

UNION-CASTLE LINE EAST AFRICAN STEAMER "LLANDOVERY CASTLE."   11,423 TONS.

LLANDOVERY CASTLE I (1914–1918)   (UCPSC 02/67)

Built by Barclay Curle, Glasgow. 195 First, 165 Second and 100 Third Class Passengers. The first ship ordered under Sir Owen Philipps' chairmanship, LLANDOVERY CASTLE set new standards for the East African service as well as for Union-Castle generally. 1918 Torpedoed and sunk 27th June by U 86, 116 miles S W Fastnet whilst fully illuminated. U 86 then shelled the lifeboats killing 234 crew and nurses, 24 survived in the captain's boat.
Sister ship: LLANSTEPHAN CASTLE

UNION-CASTLE LINE TO SOUTH AND EAST AFRICA.

THE UNION-CASTLE LINE S.S. "LLANSTEPHAN CASTLE." 11,346 TONS.

LLANSTEPHAN CASTLE (1914–1952) (UCPSC 15/170)

Built by Fairfields, Glasgow. Passenger accommodation as LLANDOVERY CASTLE I. Entire career on East African and Round Africa services. 1941 Commodore ship of the first Russian convoy, later served as an assault ship in the Burma campaign and earmarked for the invasion of Japan. 1947 Returned to commercial service September. 1952 Arrived Newport for demolition on March 1st, her career of 38 years and 10 days being the longest in the Union-Castle Line.
Sister ship: LLANDOVERY CASTLE I

CAP POLONIO (1919)

(Ship Society of S. Africa)

Built 1914 by Blohm und Voss, Hamburg, for Hamburg Sud- Amerika DGS. 1919 Surrendered 6th May. 21st June allocated to Union-Castle and sailed from Plymouth to Cape Town, arriving 18th July. 1921 resold to original owners and refitted. 1935 Broken up at Bremerhaven.

DROMORE CASTLE (1919–1941) (A. Duncan)

Built by Harland & Wolff, Greenock to modified 'B' standard design. Mainly engaged on the New York to South Africa service. 1941 Mined 12th December off the Humber whilst sailing in ballast from London to Leith to load for Russia. Sister ship: DUNDRUM CASTLE

THE UNION STEAM SHIP COMPANY'S

ROYAL MAIL TWIN SCREW STEAMER "NORMAN"
LEAVING SOUTHAMPTON FOR SOUTH AFRICA.

NORMAN II (1894–1926)   (UCPSC 17/15)

This delightful little card, undivided back, dates back to the late 1890's. The artist is unknown.

THE UNION CASTLE LINE ROYAL MAIL STEAMER "BRITON" (10248 tons)

BRITON III (1897–1926)

(UCPSC 26/41)

This card is one of a series first issued around 1905–6 and easily distinguished by the light grey hull and cloud spattered sky. Again the artist is unknown.

UNION-CASTLE LINE INTERMEDIATE STEAMER "AVONDALE CASTLE."   5,531 TONS.

AVONDALE CASTLE (1897–1912) (UCPSC 02/74)

Built by Fairfields, Glasgow. 71 First 98 second 150 Third Class Passengers. 1912 Sold 16th May, and renamed GARONNA.
1923 broken up. This card was of the second series of colour cards, artist unknown. There are at least 3 printing variations
of this series between 1906–1920.
Sister ship: TINTAGEL CASTLE I

THE UNION-CASTLE LINE ROYAL MAIL STEAMER BALMORAL CASTLE (13361 Tons)

BALMORAL CASTLE (1910–1939)   (UCPSC 08/112)

This card, by E Hamilton was issued in the late 1920's. Hamilton was responsible for a number of cards issued by Union-Castle in the 1920's and 1930's mainly featuring the mailships. Another printing of this card is in deep blue tone.

THE UNION-CASTLE Intermediate Motorship "DUNBAR CASTLE" (10000...

A spirited impression of **DUNBAR CASTLE II** by William McDowell who also painted **WARWICK CASTLE III** and **WINCHESTER CASTLE I**. Note the distinctive forward end of the superstructure. This card was issued after the war with a short description of the ship and her loss, printed in English or Afrikaans.

The UNION-CASTLE LINE M.V. " DUNVEGAN CASTLE " (15,007 tons)

DUNVEGAN CASTLE II (1936–1940)

(UCPSC 04/151)

Built by Harland & Wolff, Belfast. Passenger accommodation and service as DUNNOTTAR CASTLE II. 1940 Torpedoed West of Ireland by U 46 while serving as an Armed Merchant Cruiser. This card is by Greig in one of his more restrained moods.

Sister ship: DUNNOTTAR CASTLE II

UNION-CASTLE LINE TO SOUTH and EAST AFRICA

BLOEMFONTEIN CASTLE (1950–1959) (UCPSC 05/173)

One of the series issued in 1948–1950, this shows the Union-Castle's first one class liner in a distinctly surrealistic but not unattractive light. Unfortunately the artists name is indecipherable.

WINDSOR CASTLE III (1960–1977) (UCPSC -/190)

A little known card based on a painting by Derrick Smoothy, who painted several British & Commonwealth Group ships around 1960.

RIPLEY CASTLE (1919–1931)   (A. Duncan)

Built by Kawasaki Dockyard Co Ltd, Kobe, in 1917 as WAR SOLDIER for the Shipping Controller and purchased 23rd December 1919 by Union-Castle Line and renamed RIPLEY CASTLE. The only Japanese built Union-Castle ship and, until 1965, the only twin screw cargo vessel. 1931 Sold 2 December for demolition at Savona.

BRATTON CASTLE (1920–1932)
(A. Duncan)

Built by Armstrong, Whitworth & Co Ltd, Newcastle. Modified 'N' type fabricated steamer, having a cruiser stern. 1932 Sold and renamed PROTEUS. 1933 Renamed MOUNT TAURUS. 1942 Torpedoed 17th November in the North Atlantic voyage Liverpool to Halifax NS.
Sister ship BAMPTON CASTLE
Similar ship but with V stern BANBURY CASTLE

ARUNDEL CASTLE III (1921–1958)

(Harland & Wolff)

Laid down 25th November 1915, launched 11th September 1919 and completed April 1921 by Harland & Wolff, Belfast. The first cruiser sterned passenger ship and four funneller owned by Union-Castle. 234 First, 362 Second and 274 Third plus 300 Steerage Passengers. The photograph shows the complex array of lifeboats abaft the fourth funnel, the gantry being intended to launch them from either side.
Sister ship: WINDSOR CASTLE II

UNION-CASTLE ROYAL MAIL STEAMER "ARUNDEL CASTLE." 19,029 TONS

ARUNDEL CASTLE III (1921–1958) (UCPSC 24/143)

A broadside view of ARUNDEL CASTLE on the third series of sepia cards issued around 1935. 1936 November ARUNDEL CASTLE returned to her builders for re-engining and lengthening which took until October 1937.

UNION-CASTLE LINE TO SOUTH AND EAST AFRICA

THE UNION-CASTLE ROYAL MAIL STEAMER "ARUNDEL CASTLE" 19,216 TONS

ARUNDEL CASTLE III (1921–1958)

(UCPSC 13/179)

Appearance was completely altered and improved by her refit. Passengers 219 First, 167 Second and 194 Tourist. Served throughout the Second World War as Troopship and, in 1944 and 1945, as diplomatically protected repatriation ship exchanging wounded prisoners of war. 1948 Immigrant ship to South Africa. 1949 Commenced postwar refit. 1950 Returned to service September. 1958 withdrawn after her 211th mail voyage, sailed 30th December arriving in Hong Kong on 6th February 1959 for demolition.

SANDOWN CASTLE (1921–1950)
(A. Duncan)

Built by Short Brothers Ltd, Sunderland. Her 12 passenger accommodation was almost invariably allocated to supernumeries. 1950 Sold 30th August, after a long lay-up caused by boiler defects, for demolition at Dunston. The photograph shows her in her post 1945 livery.
Sister ship: SANDGATE CASTLE

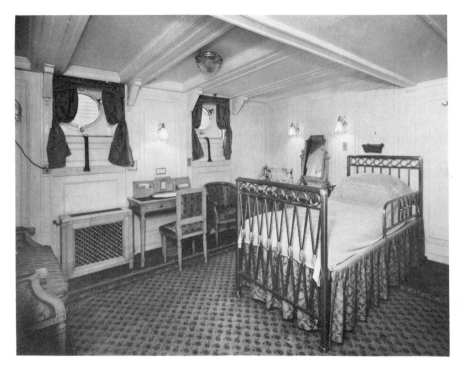

WINDSOR CASTLE II (1922–1943)   (Union-Castle)

Built by John Brown & Co Ltd, Clydebank, and launched 9th March 1921 by HRH The Prince of Wales (later Duke of Windsor), the first Royal launching of a merchant ship since Prince Albert launched GREAT BRITAIN. The photograph shows the bedroom of one of her suites and compares with that of her namesake WINDSOR CASTLE III of 1960. Sister ship: ARUNDEL CASTLE III

ROYAL MAIL STEAMER "WINDSOR CASTLE" 18.967 TONS.

WINDSOR CASTLE II (1922–1943)

(UCPSC 16/130)

This 1931 postcard shows the lines of the four funnellers to advantage. 243 First, 360 Second and 275 Third Class Passengers. In 1930 she called at Lobito to embark HRH Prince George (later Duke of Kent). 1937 Refitted as ARUNDEL CASTLE. 1943 Torpedoed by aircraft and sunk in the Mediterranean on 23rd March. 2988 troops and crew survived, but one crew man was killed.

THE UNION-CASTLE LINE S.S. ''LLANDOVERY CASTLE.''   10,639 TONS.

LLANDOVERY CASTLE II (1925–1952)   (UCPSC 06/172)

Built by Barclay Curle, Glasgow. Passengers 221 First and 186 Third. 1937 Mined 25th February near Cape Creus and was badly damaged, no casualties. 1940 23 November damaged by HE bomb and subsequent fire at Southampton. Served as Hospital ship. 1947 Returned to Round Africa service. 1952 Arrived Inverkeithing 22nd December for demolition. Sister ship: LLANDAFF CASTLE

UNION-CASTLE LINE TO SOUTH AND EAST AFRICA
ROYAL MAIL MOTOR VESSEL "CARNARVON CASTLE"   20,063 TONS

CARNARVON CASTLE II (1926–1962)   (UCPSC 09/124)

Built by Harland & Wolff, Belfast. Ordered 1923 as a steamer but redesigned to use diesel engines at the shipbuilders suggestion. Union-Castle's first 20,000 tonner and first motorship. Passengers 311 First, 276 Second and 261 Third Class Passengers.

CARNARVON CASTLE II (1926–1962)
(J. Garden)

HMS CARNARVON CASTLE shown (with Capt. Hardy DSO, RNR) entering Montevideo in December 1940 following her action with the German surface raider THOR.

THE UNION-CASTLE ROYAL MAIL MOTOR VESSEL. "CARNARVON CASTLE". 20.141 TONS.

CARNARVON CASTLE II (1926–1962) (UCPSC 01/135)

A 1950 view following CARNARVON CASTLE's postwar refit, now catering for 216 First and 401 Tourist Class passengers. In 1960 her main mast was reduced in height to simplify access to her aft hatches for dockside cranes. 1962 Delivered 12th September for demolition at Mihara.

UNION-CASTLE LINE TO SOUTH AND EAST AFRICA.

INTERMEDIATE STEAMER "LLANDAFF CASTLE." 10,786 TONS.

LLANDAFF CASTLE (1926–1942)   (UCPSC 01/135)

Built by Workman Clark & Co Ltd, Belfast. 213 First and 108 Third Class Passengers. Round Africa service. 1942 Torpedoed 30th November by U 177 off Zululand and sunk with loss of 3 lives.
Sister ship: LLANDOVERY CASTLE II

ROVUMA (1927–1949) (A. Duncan)

Built by Ardrossan Dockyard Co Ltd, Ardrossan, and employed on the East Africa feeder service between Beira and Chinde. 1949 Sold and renamed FLOREAL. 1955 Sold and renamed BOUNDARY. 1963 Broken up in Durban.

UNION-CASTLE LINE TO SOUTH AND EAST AFRICA.
M.V. "LLANGIBBY CASTLE." 11,951 TONS.

LLANGIBBY CASTLE (1929–1954)

(UCPSC 12/124)

Built by Harland & Wolff, Govan. The first motorship to circumnavigate Africa. 256 First and 198 Third Class Passengers. A planned sister ship never materialized. 1954 Broken up at Newport from July.

LLANGIBBY CASTLE (1929–1954)

(J. Fisher)

LLANGIBBY CASTLE's wartime adventures included being shelled (and knocking out the offending firearm with her own guns) during the North Africa landings and participating in the D Day Landings, but the epic was her sailing 3,400 miles minus rudder, stern and aft gun after being torpedoed by U 402 on 16th January 1942 in the North Atlantic. Here she is in the Azores a few days later awaiting an escort.

UNION-CASTLE LINE TO SOUTH AND EAST AFRICA.

INTERMEDIATE MOTOR VESSEL "DUNBAR CASTLE." 10,002 TONS.

DUNBAR CASTLE II (1930–1940)   (UCPSC 06/134)

Built by Harland & Wolff Ltd, Govan. Passengers 193 First and 250 Third Class Passengers. West Coast Intermediate service. 1938 transferred to the Round Africa service. 1940 Mined 9th January and sank off Ramsgate, with funnels and upperworks clearly visible, the wreck was finally "dispersed" in August 1949.

THE UNION-CASTLE LINE. R.M.M.V. "WINCHESTER CASTLE," 20,012 TONS.

WINCHESTER CASTLE I (1930–1960)   (UCPSC 10/195)

Built by Harland & Wolff, Belfast and re-engined in 1938, this card dates from that period. Originally twin funnelled. 1936 Ran aground 16th February on the Chesil Bank, refloated next day. Passengers after refit 256 First, 231 Second and 211 Tourist. Served as an assault ship during the war (Battle Honour Diego Suarez 1942). 1949 returned to the Mail service. 1960 Broken up at Mihara from 5th November.
Sister ship: WARWICK CASTLE III

THE UNION-CASTLE MAIL MOTORSHIP "WARWICK CASTLE." 20.445 TONS.

WARWICK CASTLE III (1931–1942)

(UCPSC 03/155))

Built by Harland & Wolff, Belfast. 260 First, 240 Second and 246 Third Class Passengers. Represented Union-Castle Line at the Silver Jubilee Royal Naval Review at Spithead in 1935. Re-engined in 1938.
Sister ship: WINCHESTER CASTLE

THE UNION-CASTLE MAIL MOTORSHIP "WARWICK CASTLE."   20,107 TONS

WARWICK CASTLE III (1931–1942)   (UCPSC 05/157E)

1938 Rejoined the mail service. 1940 October requisitioned for trooping. 1941 6th August in collision in convoy with WINDSOR CASTLE II. 1942 Torpedoed 14th November by U 413 in Convoy MFK 1 in the Atlantic whilst returning from the North African landings, broke in two and sank in heavy weather with the loss of 63 lives.

ROTHESAY CASTLE I (1935–1940)   (A. Duncan)

Built by Harland & Wolff, Belfast. Achieved 18.1 knots on trials. Escaped submarine attack early in the war by her speed.
1940 4th January ran ashore off the Isle of Islay, cargo meat from South America, and became a total loss.
"R" Class First Group Sister ship ROSLIN CASTLE III

UNION-CASTLE LINE TO SOUTH AND EAST AFRICA.

THE UNION-CASTLE ROYAL MAIL MOTOR VESSEL "STIRLING CASTLE." 25,554 TONS.

STIRLING CASTLE II (1936–1966)

(UCPSC 02/168)

Built by Harland & Wolff, Belfast. 245 First and 538 Cabin Class Passengers. 1936 Broke the 1893 record established by SCOT by $1\frac{1}{2}$ days in August. 1946 September she carried the MCC touring side to Australia for the first post war Test Match series. 1966 Sold for demolition, at Mihara.
Sister ship: ATHLONE CASTLE

ATHLONE CASTLE (1936–1965) (Harland & Wolff Ltd)

Built by Harland & Wolff, Belfast. Passenger accommodation as STIRLING CASTLE II. Their accommodation represented a complete break-away from the previously favoured "period" style of decor. This view shows a corner of the First Class Lounge. Served as a Troopship during the War.
Sister ship: STIRLING CASTLE II

THE UNION-CASTLE LINE R.M.M.V. 'ATHLONE CASTLE' 25,567 tons

ATHLONE CASTLE (1936–1965)

(UCPSC 19/197)

This superlative view, one of a series taken during her trials, shows ATHLONE CASTLE at her best. 1965 sold and arrived at Kaohsiung for demolition on 13th September. In 1968 she featured on a stamp issued by the Togolaise Republic to mark the opening of the Port of Lome. Why an ex-French colony should select a ship which had served South Africa must remain a mystery!

MOTOR VESSEL "DUNNOTTAR CASTLE." 15,007 TONS.

DUNNOTTAR CASTLE II (1936–1958)   (UCPSC 07/147)

Built by Harland & Wolff Ltd, Belfast. 258 First Class and 258 Tourist Class Passengers. Served as mailship 1936–1938 while the older mailships were re-engined. Wartime service was as an Armed Merchant Cruiser and troopship. 1958 Sold in and completely transformed by her new owners and sails 1990 as THE VICTORIA.
Sister ship: DUNVEGAN CASTLE II

WALMER CASTLE III (1936–1941)   (The late P. A. Vicary)

Built by Harland & Wolff, Belfast, for the Southampton–Hamburg weekly feeder service, replacing HANSA & EIDER. 1941 Bombed, burnt out and sank 21st September in the North Atlantic while serving as a Convoy rescue ship, amid scenes of great heroism as crew members endeavoured to save wounded survivors of other vessels previously rescued.

ROCHESTER CASTLE (1937–1970)

(Harland & Wolff)

Built by Harland & Wolff Ltd, Belfast. Launched on 11th February 1937. Note the distinctive Schat davits which identify this group from the succeeding wartime vessels of the group. 1970 Sold allegedly for demolition at Whampoa but reportedly resold and sailed on as SENG KUNG until 1983, under the Chinese flag.
"R" Class Second Group
Sister ships: ROXBURGH CASTLE I, RICHMOND CASTLE I & ROWALLAN CASTLE I

ROCHESTER CASTLE (1937–1970) (Imperial War Museum)

This photograph, taken on the evening of 15th August 1942, shows ROCHESTER CASTLE entering Grand Harbour, Valetta, at the head of the 5 surviving members of the 14 strong "Pedestal" convoy sent to raise the siege of Malta GC. Damage sustained included a 360 square foot hole abreast No 3 hold and 200 smaller holes from aerial and E-Boat attack. Capt. Richard Wren was awarded a well deserved DSO for this voyage.

R.M.M.V. "CAPETOWN CASTLE." 27,000 TONS.

CAPETOWN CASTLE (1938–1967) (UCPSC 22/146)

Built by Harland & Wolff, Belfast. 292 First and 499 Cabin Class Passengers. An enlarged version of STIRLING CASTLE II. 1960 Her career was marred by an explosion in the engine room off Las Palmas on 17th October, tragically killing 7 Engineering Officers and ratings. 1965 Transferred to an "extra" service between Southampton, Flushing and Cape Town. 1967 Broken up from 27th October at La Spezia.

UNION-CASTLE LINE. M.V. "DURBAN CASTLE." 17,388 TONS.

DURBAN CASTLE (1938–1962)   (UCPSC 19/195)

Built by Harland & Wolff, Belfast. 220 First Class and 335 Tourist Class Passengers. Served as troopship and assault ship during the war, returning to the mail service from 1947 until 1950, thereafter on the Round Africa Service. 1962 Sold and demolition commenced at Hamburg in June.
Sister ships: PRETORIA CASTLE I/WARWICK CASTLE IV

PRETORIA CASTLE I/WARWICK CASTLE IV (1939–1942,1946–1962)

(Imperial War Museum)

Built by Harland & Wolff, Belfast. Accommodation as DURBAN CASTLE. After two intermediate voyages requisitioned as an Armed Merchant Cruiser. 1942 Purchased by HM Government on 16th January. 1943 Conversion to an Escort Carrier completed 7th January 1943. Served as Training and Trials Carrier until reduced to Category B Reserve on the 31st December 1945. Repurchased 26th January 1946 by Union-Castle Line and subsequently renamed WARWICK CASTLE.
Sister ship: DURBAN CASTLE

THE UNION-CASTLE ROYAL MAIL MOTOR VESSEL "WARWICK CASTLE." 17,383 TONS.

WARWICK CASTLE IV (1946–1962)   (UCPSC 03/169)

Conversion back to a liner completed and re-entered service as Mail ship on 13th March 1947, transferring to the Round Africa in September 1950 on return to service of ARUNDEL CASTLE III. 1962 Broken up at Barcelona.

ROWALLAN CASTLE II (1943–1971)　　　　　　　　　　　　　　(Union-Castle Line)

Built by Harland & Wolff, Belfast. ROWALLAN CASTLE presents a stark profile on her wartime trials. Postwar, all three vessels of this group were remasted. 1971 Sold to Kaohsiung ship-breakers and arrived for demolition on 2nd September.
"R" Class Third Group
Sister ships: RICHMOND CASTLE II & ROXBURGH CASTLE II

(A. Duncan)

RICHMOND CASTLE II (1944–1971)

Built by Harland & Wolff, Belfast. This photograph represents the trio in their immediate postwar appearance. 1956 April towed the disabled Greek Steamer GEORGE D GRATSOS 1191 miles from north of Walvis Bay to Cape Town. 1971 Broken up at Shanghai.

"R" Class Third Group

Sister ships: ROWALLAN CASTLE II & ROXBURGH CASTLE II

ROXBURGH CASTLE II (1945–1971)   (World Ship Photo Library)

Built by Harland & Wolff, Belfast. 1947 2nd January took the first postwar Mail sailing from Southampton to South Africa.
Shown after remasting. 1971 Arrived Shanghai 19th July for demolition.
"R" Class Third Group
Sister ships: ROWALLAN CASTLE II & RICHMOND CASTLE II

UNION-CASTLE LINE TO SOUTH AND EAST AFRICA.

THE UNION-CASTLE REFRIGERATED CARGO VESSEL M.V. "RIEBEECK CASTLE." 8,355 TONS.

RIEBEECK CASTLE (1946–1971)

(UCPSC 02/182)

Built by Harland & Wolff, Belfast. Original Ministry of War Transport plans to include accommodation for 36 passengers were withdrawn in April 1945. 1971 Demolition at Kaohsiung commenced 13th December.
"R" Class Fourth Group
Sister ship: RUSTENBURG CASTLE

S.S. "GOOD HOPE CASTLE."　　9,879 TONS.

GOOD HOPE CASTLE I (1946–1959)　　　　　　　　(UCPSC 01/170)

Built by Caledon Shipbuilding & Engineering Co Ltd Dundee as EMPIRE LIFE and acquired by Union-Castle Line in March 1946. Postcard shows her shortly after registration at Cape Town on 13th July 1946. 1950 March funnel heightened. Passenger accommodation for 54 was reduced to 12 in 1952. 1959 demolition commenced September in Hong Kong.
Fast Standard Cargo Class
Sister ships: DRAKENSBERG CASTLE & KENILWORTH CASTLE III

UNION-CASTLE LINE TO SOUTH AND EAST AFRICA.

S.S. "DRAKENSBERG CASTLE." 9,905 TONS.

DRAKENSBERG CASTLE (1946–1959)

(UCPSC 02/182)

Built in 1945 by J L Thompson & Sons Ltd, Sunderland, as EMPIRE ALLENBY. 1946 Acquired by Union-Castle Line in April and registered in Cape Town on the 22nd July. This card shows her in her colours adopted in 1954. 1959 demolition commenced at Hong Kong in September.

Fast Standard Cargo Class

Sister ships: GOOD HOPE CASTLE I & KENILWORTH CASTLE III

M.V. " KENILWORTH CASTLE." 9,916 TONS.

KENILWORTH CASTLE III (1946–1967) (UCPSC 01/170)

Built in 1944 by Charles Connell & Co Ltd, Glasgow as EMPIRE WILSON. 1946 Acquired by Union-Castle Line in April. 1952 November Passenger accommodation of 36 reduced to 12. 1967 Arrived Kaohsiung for demolition November.
Fast Standard Cargo Class
Sister ships: DRAKENSBERG CASTLE & GOOD HOPE CASTLE I

THE UNION-CASTLE ROYAL MAIL STEAMER "PRETORIA CASTLE." 28,705 TONS.

PRETORIA CASTLE II (1948–1965)   (UCPSC 15/175)

Built by Harland & Wolff, Belfast. Launched by radio on the 19 August 1947 from Irene, Transvaal, by Mrs Smuts. 227 First and 478 Cabin Class Passengers. 1963 21st February she flew the flag of the Commander in Chief, South Atlantic in accordance with Royal Naval tradition following the arrival of Vice Admiral Fitzroy Talbot, CB DSO. 1966 Sold Safmarine and renamed SA ORANJE. 1975 arrived at Kaohsiung on the 2nd November for demolition.
Sister ship: EDINBURGH CASTLE III

EDINBURGH CASTLE

EDINBURGH CASTLE III (1948–1976)   (UCPSC 23/200)

Built by Harland & Wolff, Belfast. Launched 16th October 1947 by HRH Princess Margaret. Passenger accommodation identical to PRETORIA CASTLE II. 1954 Broke Cape record with an 11 day 21 hour run following engine trouble. Photograph shows appearance after remasting in 1965. 1976 Demolition commenced at Kaohsiung on 25th October. Sister ship: PRETORIA CASTLE II

BRAEMAR CASTLE II (1949–1950) (A. Duncan)

Built by Short Brothers Ltd, Sunderland, 1943 for the Ministry of War Transport and named EMPIRE DUCHESS. 1946 Chartered by Union-Castle and sailed with black hull until 1949 repainted following purchase and renamed BRAEMAR CASTLE II. The last coal burner in the Union-Castle fleet. 1950 Sold, renamed KING JAMES. 1958 sold and renamed TYNE BREEZE. 1963 Sold, renamed CATHAY TRADER. 1964 Sold and renamed PEARL LIGHT. 1966 Sold, renamed HABIB MARIKAR. A troublesome career ended on Lincoln Island when she grounded and became a total loss.

THE UNION-CASTLE LINE M.V. "BLOEMFONTEIN CASTLE" 18,400 TONS.

BLOEMFONTEIN CASTLE (1950–1959)   (UCPSC 01/179)

Built by Harland & Wolff, Belfast. 727 One Class passengers. Hull and engines identical to DURBAN CASTLE. Originally intended as an immigrant ship. 1953 8th January rescued complement of Dutch mv KLIPFONTEIN after that vessel sank off Mozambique. 1959 Sold November and renamed PATRIS. 1979 Resold and renamed MEDITERRANEAN ISLAND, and in 1981 MEDITERRANEAN SUN. 1987 Renamed TERRA in August, and demolition commenced at Gadani Beach on 11th October.

UNION-CASTLE LINE TO SOUTH AND EAST AFRICA

THE UNION-CASTLE LINE S.S. "RHODESIA CASTLE," 17,038 TONS

RHODESIA CASTLE (1951–1967)   (UCPSC 06/187)

Built by Harland & Wolff, Belfast. Passenger accommodation 530 Cabin class. 1960 Refitted and partially air conditioned, when her funnel was fitted with a domed top (as shown). 1967 Sold for demolition at Kaohsiung, work commenced 1st November.

Sister ships: KENYA CASTLE & BRAEMAR CASTLE III

KENYA CASTLE (1952–1967) (World Ship Photo Library)

Built by Harland & Wolff, Belfast. Passenger accommodation as RHODESIA CASTLE. Round Africa and East Africa service. 1961 refitted as RHODESIA CASTLE. 1967 Sold for service as cruise ship, passenger accommodation extended, and renamed AMERIKANIS (as shown). 1990 still in service.
Sister ships: RHODESIA CASTLE & BRAEMAR CASTLE III

THE UNION-CASTLE LINE S.S. "BRAEMAR CASTLE"   17,029 TONS

BRAEMAR CASTLE III (1952–1966)   (UCPSC 05/182)

Built by Harland & Wolff Ltd, Belfast. 526 Cabin Class passengers. 1955 June Temporarily replaced STIRLING CASTLE on mail service, steamed from Southampton to Cape Town in 13 days $17\frac{3}{4}$ hours (18.09 knots), a record for an intermediate. 1959 Ran ashore in gale in Algeciras Bay 1 December, refloated next day. 1961 Refitted and domed funnel added. 1966 arrived Faslane 24 January for demolition.
Sister ships: RHODESIA CASTLE & KENYA CASTLE

UNION-CASTLE LINE TO SOUTH AND EAST AFRICA.

THE UNION-CASTLE LINE M.V. "TANTALLON CASTLE" 7448 TONS.

TANTALLON CASTLE III (1954–1971)   (UCPSC 01/182)

Built by Harland & Wolff, Belfast. 12 passengers until 1963. Launched on 22nd October 1953, 15 days after the centenary of the Company. 1971 Sold and renamed ARIS II. 1972 Renamed ARIS. 1978 Demolition at Aioi commenced 5th September.
Sister ship: TINTAGEL CASTLE II

"PENDENNIS CASTLE"

PENDENNIS CASTLE (1958–1976)   (UCPSC 15/185)

Built by Harland & Wolff, Belfast. The last Union-Castle ship built by them after 65 years. Originally planned as a sister ship of EDINBURGH CASTLE III, but lengthened and otherwise improved whilst on the stocks. 164 First Class and 473 Tourist Class passengers. In 1968 and 1969 steamed in both directions in 10½ days (23.75 knots) to set the final Union-Castle records. 1976 June sold and renamed OCEAN QUEEN. 1977 Renamed SINDBAD later SINDBAD I.1980 Broken up at Kaohsiung in April after 3¾ years laid up.

ROTHERWICK CASTLE (1959–1975)

(A. Duncan)

Built by Greenock Dockyard Co Ltd, Greenock. 11th October 1965 rescued Herr Langi Faulker in the Straits of Gibraltar after his amphibious car proved better suited to dry land. 1975 Sold and renamed SEA FORTUNE. 1980 Renamed SILVER RAYS. 1983 broken up at Chittagong from January.
Sister ship: ROTHESAY CASTLE II (distinguishable by taller funnel)

THE UNION-CASTLE ROYAL MAIL STEAMER "WINDSOR CASTLE" 38,000 TONS

WINDSOR CASTLE III (1960–1977)

(UCPSC 16/182)

Built by Cammell Laird & Co (Shipbuilding) Ltd, Birkenhead. Launched by HM Queen Elizabeth the Queen Mother on 23 June 1959. 191 First and 591 Tourist Class passengers. (some interchangeable). 1965 Inaugurated $11\frac{1}{2}$ Mail schedule on 16th July. 1977 took final Union-Castle passenger sailing on 12th August from Southampton. Sold October and renamed MARGARITA L. 1990 In service as an accommodation ship at Jeddah.

WINDSOR CASTLE III (1960–1977)   (Union-Castle Line)

This view of a First Class suite contrasts with a corresponding illustration of WINDSOR CASTLE II (qv).

WINDSOR CASTLE III (1960–1977) (Union-Castle Line)

The First Class Dining Saloon by day, with a mural of Windsor Castle.

UNION-CASTLE — Die Groot Manier Om Na Europa Te Reis.

TRANSVAAL CASTLE (1962–1966)   (UCPSC 05/199A)

Built by John Brown & Co Ltd, Clydebank. 740 Hotel Class passengers. 1966 Sold to Safmarine and renamed SA VAAL.
1977 Sold and renamed FESTIVALE. This postcard is one of four issued in 1962 (artist Derrick Smoothy) captioned
alternately in English and Afrikaans. 1990 In service as cruise liner.

KINNAIRD CASTLE (1962–1975)

(Fotoship)

Built 1956 by Greenock Dockyard Co Ltd, Greenock for the Clan Line Steamers Ltd and named CLAN ROSS. 1961 Sold to Safmarine and renamed SOUTH AFRICAN SCIENTIST. 1962 Sold back to Clan Line and renamed KINNAIRD CASTLE. 1975 Sold and renamed NAZEER. 1978 Broken up at Gadani beach from April.

Similar ship: KINPURNIE CASTLE I. Both vessels were typical Clan Line steamers of the 1950's. Neither was actually owned by Union-Castle despite carrying "Castle" names.

THE UNION-CASTLE CARGO MAIL SHIP "SOUTHAMPTON CASTLE" 13,152 TONS.

SOUTHAMPTON CASTLE (1965–1978)   (UCPSC 01/182)

Built by Swan Hunter & Wigham Richardson Ltd, Wallsend. Speed in excess of 26 knots made her the fastest cargo liner in service. 1967 equipped to carry 12 passengers plus deck passengers for the Ascension and St Helena service. 1977 Sailed 11th October on the final Cape Town to Southampton sailing in the Mail service, arriving 20th October. 1978 Sold and renamed FRANCA C. 1984 Sold renamed FRANCA and arrived Dalian 19th January for demolition.
Sister ship: GOOD HOPE CASTLE II

DOVER CASTLE III (1965–1981)

(A. Duncan)

Built by Greenock Dockyard Co Ltd, Greenock. Originally named CLAN RANALD. 1977 January renamed DOVER CASTLE. 1979 May renamed DOVER UNIVERSAL. 1981 Sold June and renamed GOLDEN SEA. 1985 Broken up at Gadani beach from 11th May.
Sister ships: CLAN RAMSAY/WINCHESTER CASTLE II, CLAN ROBERTSON/BALMORAL CASTLE III, both owned by Union-Castle, and CLAN ROSS/KINPURNIE CASTLE II owned until 1976 by Houston Line Ltd

GOOD HOPE CASTLE II (1966–1978)   (R. Pabst)

Built by Swan Hunter & Wigham Richardson Ltd, Wallsend. 1967 Refitted to carry 12 passengers. 1973 Caught fire 29 June 35 miles SE of Ascension Island, eventually towed to Santander and repair completed May 1974. 1978 Sold and renamed PAOLA C. 1984 Sold and renamed PAOLA arrived Shanghai 27 July for demolition.
Sister ship: SOUTHAMPTON CASTLE

REINA DEL MAR (Chartered 1964–1973) (Owned 1973–1975)   (A. Duncan)

Built by Harland & Wolff for the Pacific Steam Navigation Co Ltd. 1964 Chartered by Union-Castle for full time cruising carrying 998 passengers. 1973 Purchased but sold for demolition 18 months later in 1975 after the oil fuel price increases. Demolition at Kaohsiung commenced 10th December.

ACKNOWLEDGEMENTS AND BIBLIOGRAPHY

Information in this volume is extracted from extensive records of the Union-Castle Line prepared from Lloyd's Register with assistance from Pat Tye, Jean Hood, Barbara Jones and Sandra Scott, from the Ship's Certificates in the Public Record Office, from the Guildhall Library, and from the records of the Union-Castle Mail Steamship Company Ltd, and from that company, particularly Charles Lemon and June Foster. I am also grateful to Capt J. P. Smythe for the information on PRETORIA CASTLE II.

Further information has been obtained from *Sea Breezes*, *Ships Monthly*, *Marine News*, *Flotsam & Jetsam* and numerous newspaper cuttings. Marischal Murray's two books, *Ships and South Africa* (OUP 1933) and *Union-Castle Chronicle* (Longmans 1953) are essential reading. Sawyer & Mitchell's *The Cape Run* (1984) is useful for the post 1953 period, while Laurence Dunn's *Ships of the Union-Castle Line* (1954) covers further detail of the fleet. The memoirs of George Young, former Shipping Editor of the *Cape Times*, *Salt in my Blood* (J. F. Midgeley 1975) and *Ships that Pass* (J. F. Midgeley 1976) include much worthwhile information not otherwise readily available.

Finally my thanks are due to my printers, Page Bros (Norwich) Ltd, and to Rosemary Klein and Sarah Lee of North Walsham, Norfolk, who typed the manuscript.

For the reader seeking more specialized information the following are recommended:

1. *Victorian Shipping, Business and Imperial Policy, Donald Currie, the Castle Line and South Africa*, by Dr Andrew Porter. (The Royal Historical Society Studies in History No 49, ISBN 0 86193 205 6.)
   An erudite and comprehensive study of Sir Donald Currie's business life.

2. *The South African Shipping Question 1886–1914*, by V. E. Solomon. (The Historical Publication Society, ISBN 0620 06017 4.)
   The early years of South and South East African Shipping Conference and the Deferred Rebates Dispute.

3. *The Politics of the South Africa Run*, by G. R. Berridge. (Clarendon Press, Oxford, ISBN 0 19 827484 X.)
   The relationships of the Union-Castle Line and the South African Government after 1945.

4. *A Business of National Importance*, by E. Green & M. Moss (Methuen, ISBN 0416 32220 4.)
   A thorough study of the collapse of the Royal Mail Group.

5. *Shipbuilders to the World*, by E. Green and M. Moss. (The Black Staff Press, ISBN 085640 343 1.)
   The history of Harland & Wolff Ltd, builders of many Union-Castle liners.

INDEX

Notes

1. The notation in Roman numerals following a ship's name indicates that the ship is the first, second, etc, vessel of that name in the fleet. No numeral is shown where only one ship bore the name in question. Because the index lists only ships featured in this book there are otherwise inexplicable gaps.

2. Dimensions are Registered Length × Beam × Depth, or for vessels marked with an asterisk, Overall Length × Beam × Load Draft. All dimensions to the nearest foot.

3. Gross Tonnage is as completed or as rebuilt (see note 7). It should be noted that this figure varies by subsequent modification or change of rules.

4. Engine type is indicated as follows:
   Reciprocating
   S = Simple; C = Compound; T = Triple Expansion; Q = Quadruple Expansion followed by the number of cylinders.
   Diesel
   D = Oil Engines. 2SC/4SC indicates 2 or 4 stroke cycle.
   DA/SA indicates Double or Single Action.
   Turbine
   Tur indicates Steam Turbine, preceded by SR (Single Reduction Gearing), or DR (Double Reduction Gearing).
   General
   The prefix 2 × indicates two sets of engines driving twin screws.

5. Horse Power stated is:

   (a) For Reciprocating Engines - Indicated, or marked by an asterisk, Registered.
   (b) For Diesel - Brake
   (c) For Turbines - Shaft.

6. Speed is the best average maintainable in Union-Castle service by the ship in her earlier years over a voyage experiencing fair but not necessarily excellent weather conditions. As a rough guide it is generally around 2 knots in excess of normal service requirements.

7. In the case of ships substantially modified during their careers amended particulars are re-stated immediately below the original entry.

	Dimensions	Tonnage	Machinery	Power	Speed	Page
ANGLIAN II	314 × 36 × 26	2206	C 2Cyl	*270	8	13
(Re-engined)	314 × 36 × 26	2246	T 3Cyl	*309	8½	
ARMADALE CASTLE	570 × 64 × 39	12973	2×Q 4Cyl	12500	17	47, 48
AROS CASTLE	392 × 49 × 18	4459	T 3Cyl	2500	10	43
ARUNDEL CASTLE III	*661 × 72 × 33	19023	2×SR Tur	14000	16	75, 76,
(Rebuilt)	*687 × 72 × 33	19118	2×SR Tur	24000	19	77
ATHENIAN	365 × 46 × 29	3877	C 2Cyl	*600	13	17
(Re-engined)	365 × 46 × 29	3877	T 3Cyl	*649	14	
ATHLONE CASTLE	*725 × 82 × 32	25564	2×D 2SCDA	24000	19½	95, 96
AVONDALE CASTLE	425 × 50 × 30	5531	T 3Cyl	3500	12½	67
BALMORAL CASTLE II	570 × 65 × 39	13361	2×Q 4Cyl	12500	17	54, 56, 68
BLOEMFONTEIN CASTLE	*595 × 76 × 29	18400	2×D 2SCDA	16000	17½	71, 115
BRAEMAR CASTLE I	450 × 52 × 22	6266	Q 4Cyl	4400	13½	35
BRAEMAR CASTLE II	*446 × 56 × 27	7067	T 3Cyl	2500	10	114
BRAEMAR CASTLE III	*576 × 74 × 28	17029	2×DR Tur	14400	18	118
BRATTON CASTLE	412 × 56 × 34	6696	T 3Cyl	2500	9½	74
BRITON III	530 × 60 × 36	10248	2×T 3Cyl	10500	16½	33, 66
CAPETOWN CASTLE	*734 × 82 × 32	27000	2×D 2SCDA	24000	19	101
CAP POLONIO	638 × 72 × 39	20597	2×T 4Cyl+Tur	20000	11	63
CARISBROOKE CASTLE II	485 × 56 × 24	7626	Q 4Cyl	9000	17½	34
CARNARVON CASTLE II	*661 × 73 × 33	20063	2×D 4SCDA	13000	16	82
(Rebuilt)	*686 × 73 × 33	20122	2×D 2SCDA	24000	20	83, 84
CAWDOR CASTLE	415 × 51 × 28	6235	2×T 3Cyl	3400	11½	44
CLUNY CASTLE II	419 × 50 × 28	5147	2×T 3Cyl	2900	11	45
DOVER CASTLE II	476 × 57 × 32	8260	2×Q 4Cyl	5200	13½	50
DOVER CASTLE III	*529 × 68 × 28	10541	D 7Cyl 2SCSA	10350	17½	128
DRAKENSBERG CASTLE	*500 × 64 × 30	9904	DR Tur	6800	14½	110
DROMORE CASTLE	400 × 52 × 28	5242	T 3Cyl	2500	10	64
DUNBAR CASTLE II	471 × 61 × 30	10002	2×D 4SCSA	6300	14	69, 89
DUNLUCE CASTLE	475 × 57 × 32	8114	2×Q 4Cyl	5200	13½	52
DUNNOTTAR CASTLE I	420 × 50 × 25	5465	T 3Cyl	6700	15	20
DUNNOTTAR CASTLE II	*560 × 72 × 28	15007	2×D 2SCDA	9500	15½	97
DUNROBIN CASTLE	342 × 38 × 28	2811	C 2Cyl	1400	10	14
DUNVEGAN CASTLE I	450 × 51 × 24	5958	T 3Cyl	7000	15½	28

	Dimensions	Tonnage	Machinery	Power	Speed	Page
DUNVEGAN CASTLE II	*560 × 72 × 28	15007	2×D 2SCDA	9500	15½	70
DURBAN CASTLE	*595 × 76 × 29	17388	2×D 2SCDA	16000	17½	97
DURHAM CASTLE	475 × 57 × 32	8217	2×Q 4Cyl	5200	13½	49
EDINBURGH CASTLE I	335 × 38 × 28	2678	C 2Cyl	1000	9	11
EDINBURGH CASTLE II	570 × 65 × 39	13326	2×Q 4Cyl	12500	17	57
EDINBURGH CASTLE III	*747 × 84 × 32	28705	2×DR Tur	35000	22½	113
FLORENCE	189 × 25 × 14	616	S 2Cyl	340	8	12
(Rebuilt)	219 × 25 × 14	694	C 2Cyl	*70	8	
GAIKA	430 × 52 × 29	6287	2×T 3Cyl	2750	11½	31
GALEKA	440 × 53 × 30	6767	2×T 3Cyl	2800	11½	39
GALICIAN/GLENART CASTLE	440 × 53 × 30	6757	2×T 3Cyl	2800	11½	42
GALWAY CASTLE	452 × 56 × 31	7988	2×Q 4Cyl	3750	12½	60
GARTH CASTLE II	453 × 54 × 30	7606	2×Q 4Cyl	3250	12	56
GASCON	430 × 52 × 29	6288	2×T 3Cyl	2750	11½	30
GERMAN II/GLENGORM CASTLE	440 × 53 × 22	6763	2×T 3Cyl	2800	11½	36
GLOUCESTER CASTLE	453 × 56 × 31	7999	2×Q 4Cyl	3750	12½	58
GOOD HOPE CASTLE I	*494 × 64 × 30	9879	DR Tur	6800	14½	109
GOOD HOPE CASTLE II	*593 × 77 × 31	13152	2×D2SASC	34750	26	129
GOORKHA	430 × 52 × 29	6287	2×T 3Cyl	2750	11½	32
GOTH	400 × 47 × 27	4738	2×T 3Cyl	2200	11	23
GOTHLAND	252 × 32 × 17	1482	C 2Cyl	*150	9	10
GRANTULLY CASTLE I	360 × 44 × 29	3489	C 2Cyl	*550	11	
(Re-engined)	360 × 44 × 29	3453	T 3Cyl	*550	12	15
GRANTULLY CASTLE II	451 × 54 × 31	7606	2×Q 4Cyl	3250	12	53
GUELPH	400 × 47 × 27	4917	2×T 3Cyl	2200	11	25
GUILDFORD CASTLE	452 × 56 × 31	7995	2×Q 4Cyl	3750	12½	59
KENILWORTH CASTLE II	570 × 65 × 39	12975	2×Q 4Cyl	12500	17	51
KENILWORTH CASTLE III	*497 × 64 × 30	9916	D 2SCDA	6800	14½	111
KENYA CASTLE	*576 × 74 × 28	17041	2×DR Tur	14400	18	117
KILDONAN CASTLE	515 × 59 × 35	9652	2×Q 4Cyl	11800	16½	38
KINFAUNS CASTLE II	515 × 59 × 35	9664	2×Q 4Cyl	9800	16½	37
KINNAIRD CASTLE	*503 × 66 × 27	7698	DR Tur	9400	16½	126

	Dimensions	Tonnage	Machinery	Power	Speed	Page
LLANDAFF CASTLE	471 × 61 × 39	10786	2×Q 4Cyl	5500	14	85
LLANDOVERY CASTLE I	500 × 63 × 37	11423	2×Q 4Cyl	5800	14	61
LLANDOVERY CASTLE II	471 × 61 × 39	10609	2×Q 4Cyl	5500	14	81
LLANGIBBY CASTLE	*524 × 66 × 27	11951	2×D 4SCSA	8500	15	87, 88
LLANSTEPHAN CASTLE	500 × 63 × 37	11293	2×Q 4Cyl	5800	14	62
NORMAN II	491 × 53 × 33	7537	2×T 3Cyl	9000	16	26, 27, 65
PEMBROKE CASTLE II	400 × 43 × 21	3639	C 2Cyl	3200	12	9
PENDENNIS CASTLE	*763 × 84 × 32	28582	2×DR Tur	42500	24	120
PRETORIA CASTLE I	*595 × 76 × 29	17392	2×D 2SCDA	16000	17½	103, 104
PRETORIA CASTLE II	*747 × 84 × 32	28705	2×DR Tur	35000	22½	112
REINA DEL MAR	*601 × 78 × 20	20225	2×DR Tur	18700	18	130
RHODESIA CASTLE	*567 × 74 × 28	17041	2×DR Tur	14400	18	116
RICHMOND CASTLE II	*474 × 63 × 29	7971	D 2SCDA	8000	16	106
RIEBEECK CASTLE	*474 × 63 × 29	8322	D 2SCDA	8000	15½	108
RIPLEY CASTLE	445 × 58 × 31	7521	2×T 3Cyl	3200	11	73
ROCHESTER CASTLE	*474 × 63 × 29	7795	D 2SCDA	8000	16	99, 100
ROMAN I	267 × 32 × 24	1282	S 2Cyl	*220	8½	
(Rebuilt)	321 × 32 × 24	1851	C 2Cyl	*274	9	9
ROSLIN CASTLE II	380 × 48 × 31	4280	C 2Cyl	3350	13½	
(Rebuilt)	393 × 48 × 31	4487	T 3Cyl	5700	15	18
ROTHERWICK CASTLE	*520 × 66 × 28	9650	D 2SCSA	9500	16½	121
ROTHESAY CASTLE I	*443 × 61 × 29	7016	D 2SCDA	8000	17	93
ROVUMA	212 × 55 × 19	1289	2×T 3Cyl	730	8½	86
ROWALLAN CASTLE II	*474 × 63 × 29	7950	D 2SCDA	8000	16	105
ROXBURGH CASTLE II	474 × 63 × 29	8003	D 2SCDA	8000	16	107
SANDOWN CASTLE	425 × 56 × 36	7607	DR Tur	3200	11	78
SAXON II	245 × 32 × 24	1141	S 2Cyl	*220	8½	8
SAXON IV	570 × 64 × 38	12385	2×Q 4Cyl	11800	17	40, 41
SCOT	477 × 55 × 26	6844	2×T 3Cyl	11626	17½	21
(Rebuilt)	531 × 55 × 26	7815	2×T 3Cyl	11626	17½	22
SOUTHAMPTON CASTLE	*593 × 77 × 31	13152	2×D 2SCSA	34720	26	127
STIRLING CASTLE II	*725 × 82 × 32	25550	2×D 2SCDA	24000	19½	94

	Dimensions	Tonnage	Machinery	Power	Speed	Page
TANTALLON CASTLE II	440 × 50 × 24	5636	Q 4Cyl	8000	16	24
TANTALLON CASTLE III	*495 × 66 × 28	7448	D 2SCDA	8000	16	119
TINTAGEL CASTLE I	425 × 50 × 30	5531	T 3Cyl	3500	12½	29
TRANSVAAL CASTLE	*760 × 90 × 32	32697	2×DR Tur	40000	23½	125
TROJAN	364 × 43 × 29	3555	C 2Cyl	3500	13½	16
(Re-engined)	364 × 43 × 29	3471	T 3Cyl	3500	13½	
WALMER CASTLE II	570 × 64 × 39	12546	2×Q 4Cyl	11800	17	46
WALMER CASTLE III	236 × 39 × 13	906	D 2SCDA	2400	14	119
WARWICK CASTLE III	651 × 75 × 37	20445	2×D 4SCDA	13000	16	91
(Rebuilt)	651 × 75 × 37	20107	2×D 2SCDA	24000	20	92
WARWICK CASTLE IV See PRETORIA CASTLE I						104
WINCHESTER CASTLE I	*657 × 75 × 32	20109	2×D 4SCDA	13000	16	
(Rebuilt)	*657 × 75 × 32	20012	2×D 2SCDA	24000	20	91
WINDSOR CASTLE II	*661 × 72 × 33	18967	2×SR Tur	14000	16	79, 80
(Rebuilt)	*686 × 72 × 33	19141	2×SR Tur	24000	20	
WINDSOR CASTLE III	*783 × 92 × 32	37640	2×DR Tur	45000	23½	72, 122–124